# Kid's Book -
# A Theory of Emotions

## Cassandra Wilson

CASSANDRA WILSON

ISBN #978-1-988949-02-4

CASSANDRA WILSON

Dedication: I dedicate this book to all kids learning to understand their emotions.

Contents: A teacher's or parent's reading book to helping your students understand love through balanced emotions. Follow through by reading all the pages of this book to the games at the end.

# Acknowledgements

I have had many teachers: My wonderful father and mother, family members and special friends, Freda Clark of Vancouver, Desiree Rainbird of South Africa, Marise Fennel of Ireland, Paul Scott of Gibson's B.C. and Kathie Scott and Angela Heit from Ontario, to name a few.

# New News!

## Emotions are our friends!

Our emotions are tools of awareness and understanding of ourselves. They are the keys to personal growth and self-love - but many people ignore these precious tools, suppress them or deny them! It's a strange thing, but over centuries, humans have believed emotions to be a nuisance, a weakness or getting in the way of thought. As a result of this pressing down and ignoring emotions, they have become misunderstood.

These days, thankfully, humans are becoming aware of their emotions and respecting them, and even understanding them. It's a beautiful new chance for humans to learn about and accept emotions. Its a wonderful development, so if you are reading this now, Bravo! You are waking up to even greater personal power and understanding and developing your self-love.

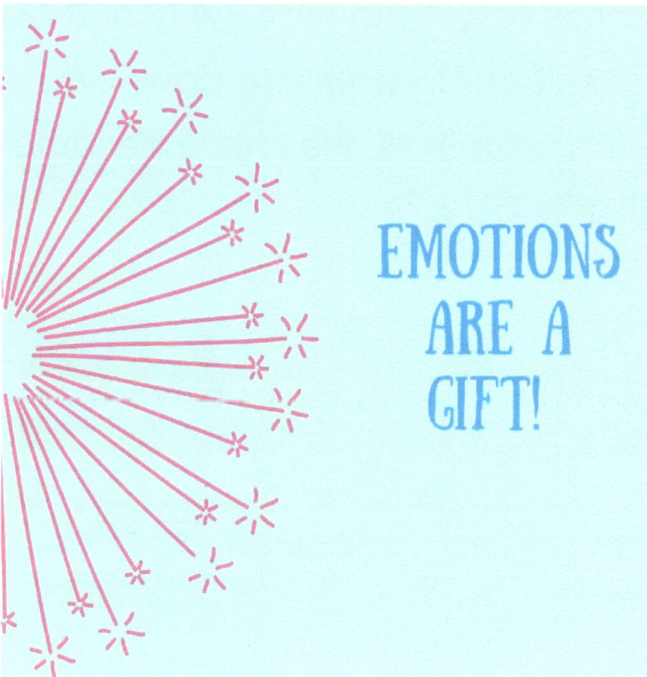

EMOTIONS ARE A GIFT!

Did you know there is a range of emotion, like a musical scale? The scale goes from JOY which is at the top all the way down to FEAR which is at the bottom. Humans experience all emotions during life, just like all the notes on a scale. In your life, you will experience all emotions, as if your body is singing a song! It is a song, a song of Life.

Of course, we hope to sing mostly happy songs, and feel good feelings. But sometimes we face situations where we feel emotions on the lower end of the scale, and it's important how we respond to those lower notes. Just as the musical notes are all different - so are our emotions! Even if we feel Fear, and it's uncomfortable, it's still valuable! Feelings change and shift so we feel many different feelings during the day. So if your emotion is uncomfortable, just wait.

Listen to your feeling, receive its message and then it will fade away. The job of any emotion is delivering to you an important message. If you receive the message, the job of the emotion is done and it will disappear.

It's usually a message about yourself, how you want to feel, how you want to be treated, what your preferences are, and what is true to you. It's very useful to know these things about yourself, now and as you grow into an adult.

## THE EMOTIONAL GUIDANCE SCALE

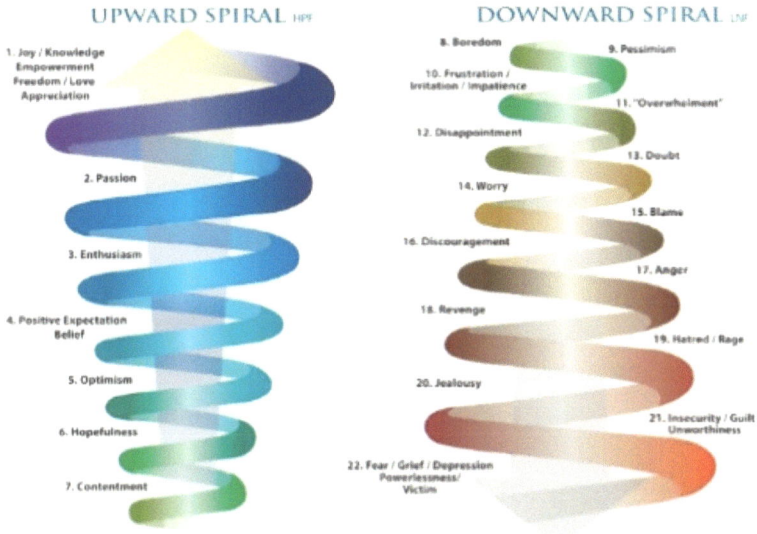

**UPWARD SPIRAL** HFF                          **DOWNWARD SPIRAL** LFF

1. Joy / Knowledge
   Empowerment
   Freedom / Love
   Appreciation

8. Boredom

9. Pessimism

10. Frustration /
    Irritation / Impatience

11. "Overwhelment"

12. Disappointment

2. Passion

13. Doubt

14. Worry

15. Blame

3. Enthusiasm

16. Discouragement

17. Anger

4. Positive Expectation
   Belief

18. Revenge

19. Hatred / Rage

5. Optimism

20. Jealousy

6. Hopefulness

21. Insecurity / Guilt
    Unworthiness

22. Fear / Grief / Depression
    Powerlessness/
    Victim

7. Contentment

The List of Emotions shown here is on the next page. Source is Abraham-Hicks.

Emotional Scale - Read down the list and back up again.

1. Joy/Peace/Love/Freedom

2. Passion

3. Enthusiasm

4. Positive Expectation/Belief

5. Optimism

6. Hopefulness

7. Contentment

8. Boredom

9. Pessimism

10. Frustration/Irritation/Impatience

11. Overwhelmed

12. Disappointment

13. Doubt

14. Worry

15. Blame

16. Discouragement

17. Anger

18. Revenge

19. Hatred/Rage

20. Jealousy

21. Insecurity/Guilt/Unworthiness

22. Fear/Grief/Depression/Despair/Powerlessness

WOW! What a range of feelings! Did you hear the difference? Did your voices change while you read the words out loud?

These are the emotional notes we feel in life. As you can see, each emotion has a friend on either side - one is a better feeling, and one is a worse feeling. Keep climbing up the scale until you feel better, listening to your emotions along the way. Learn the message the emotion has for you, then move up to a better feeling!

You can imagine your emotional self being like a garden. Sometimes rocks emerge in a garden, just like emotions, hidden there until they appear. When we see the rock or emotion on the surface, we can pick it up, look at it, wonder about it then release it from the garden. Sometimes the rocks are big and sometimes they are small. They all have a story to tell. When you listen to yourself, you feel better.

As we take care of our emotional 'gardens', more plants, flowers, fruits or vegetables can grow. We are the farmers of our emotional selves and personal growth. Just as we listen, learn and clear away emotions, more of our beautiful selves can grow, just like the plants in the garden.

You are in charge of how you feel.

FIRST, RECEIVE THE MESSAGE IN YOUR EMOTION. THEN, YOU CAN LET IT GO.

You may be wondering how to receive the message in your emotion. You can receive the message by listening to your quiet self. Learn how to create personal time where you can listen to your quiet self and hear your inner messages. If you listen to yourself in silence, you will hear the message waiting for you.

Your emotions are messages from your heart, or from your soul. When you listen, you can feel them in your body, too! Emotions are there for a good reason. The best thing for you to do when you feel an emotion, is take time to understand it. What is the message in it? What has happened that has caused you to feel this way? Often we feel emotions IN RESPONSE to something that has happened - something someone has said or done, or something we see happening can make us feel an emotion.

Lots of times others make us feel JOY! That is wonderful and we can say Thank You to that person or that situation.

But sometimes we can feel emotions that make us cry or feel sad, or any of the emotions on the lower end of the scale. That's okay, too. It's okay because it's a chance for us to learn about ourselves. We feel emotions IN RESPONSE to events or experiences and it's our job to find out why we feel a certain way. What is the real reason? What is the belief we have about that? What is there for us to learn about our feeling?

It's best if we try to discover the messages our heart or soul has sent us FIRST. Afterward, we may decide to talk with another person. We talk with ourselves first, because we may find the treasure in ourselves and then we don't have to talk with another about it.

# Important!

**Triggers!** Triggers are when something someone does or says makes you feel a strong emotion! Strong emotions are the result of a past memory or pain that is getting attention now.

For example: **Your friend says something not nice about an older lady walking by. It *triggers* you, then you feel upset (a sign of feeling a lower emotion) and begin to cry. You are 'triggered' with emotion when you react instead of a responding.**

*Here is your chance! A letter from your soul!*

You can take a moment to sit quietly and ask yourself, Why?

When you ask yourself Why, you realize its because you miss your Grandma who passed away a few months ago. You are feeling Grief (#22). You still had a feeling of grief in your body from missing your Grandma and you realize that is why you are crying. You can allow your lower emotion to flow through you, remembering your loving Grandma and the times you shared together, letting tears fall and catching them with a tissue or your fingers. Then, after a few deep breaths, you feel better because you still feel her love, you still have happy memories and you decide to send a sweet Hello and blow a kiss to your Grandma in heaven.

Secondly, it may be that your friend doesn't yet understand how to respect her elders, but that is her lesson and learning. You could choose to say nothing to your friend, Or you could say honestly, "I miss my Grandma and it makes me cry sometimes." Your friend may learn from you to love her elders, and learn to speak more kindly about older people or she may keep that

information to understand later. You don't need to teach her anything, but you've done a good job in respecting your feelings, and also honouring your friend's path.

Emotions are very important because they show us the root of our beliefs. The beautiful thing about our emotions is that they hold stories from our past. When we ask Why we feel emotions, we begin to learn the stories buried in our roots and discover the mystery of our selves that makes us unique.

Emotions can be confusing and difficult to understand *unless* we sit quietly to listen to the message. It may be like peeling an onion, with layers into the centre of our feeling but the taste of onion once its cooked makes meals much more flavourful!

Our emotions once understood, are wonderful! Feeling is part of life. Let's get to know our good friends emotions.

One important thing about emotions, is that if you don't listen to them within a few days, they can affect other areas of your life. It is best to use your energy to help you grow, and listen to your emotions when they come.

An easy way to do this when others are around is to excuse yourself to the bathroom. There you can have some quiet time just in case you need it.

We all want to live a happy life, feeling the upper emotions most of the time. But, sometimes you will meet someone who struggles to hear or understand the messages of their emotions. They need more love and understanding from their friends or family, and if someone in your life is showing you their emotions loudly too often, they need understanding and encouragement to listen, too.

We can help our friends or family member by 1) listening, (without adding our opinion) 2) reframing (which is saying the same story back to them in different words) or we can 3) give comfort in a hug or by holding someone's hand, (you decide the action) whatever you are comfortable with.

These three ways will help in any situation - you just have to decide which one to use. Many of you know how to listen, because you are caring. Showing others caring is just as important. We all must grow in kindness to one another, and this is how -

1. Respecting ourselves,

2. Respecting each other, and

3. Learning what that means.

Respect means honouring Boundaries. It's important to ask if you don't know where someone's boundary is, an invisible line around your body and your feelings. Boundaries make us feel safe.

We never want to make anyone uncomfortable under any circumstances, so we never push another's boundaries to do something they don't want to.

You can always ask - Is this okay for you? Are you enjoying yourself? What could be better? Sometimes you have to ask a person a few times to get an answer, but it's worth asking because you'll both learn something.

Decide today that you'll make the transition to kindness and clarity no matter what the challenges to the best of your ability? Could you imagine the kinder world we could create if you really cared about creating it?!

Play a Game!

- Call out an Emotion from the Emotions Scale and talk about it. What do we know about it?

- What types of sentences might be spoken with someone feeling this?

- What could we do to help them feel better?

- What could we do for ourselves if we have this feeling?

- Could we talk to someone? Who?

- Who helps us the best when we need a hug or an extra hand in feeling better?

- How does this person help you feel better? Describe using Emotions.

- Share with the person next to you how you overcame an emotion by accepting it, allowing it, acknowledging it.

Share some ideas!

- Share with the class the kindest answer. Share stories you have heard from other people.

- Make Bristol board wall charts about the emotions, one student choosing one emotion and decorating it, learning about it, then sharing about it. Then assemble emotions for the wall.

- Card Games: Make two cards of each emotion and play matching games. Play Fish and say something helpful about that emotion.

- Share about a time when someone had a different emotion then you expected and how you responded,.

- Make a person on a Bristol board and decorate her/him with kind sentences, actions and rewards.

- Describe how you would parent someone like you around emotions.

# The End

Contact the Author Cassandra Lea Wilson

cassandraleawilson@gmail.com

www.ingramcontent.com/pod-product-compliance
Lightning Source LLC
LaVergne TN
LVHW010023070426
835508LV00001B/33